This book belongs to:

If lost, please contact:

Dedication

To my mother, Christine. Who told me in my girlhood that she wished for me to go further, do more, and be better than she is. A beautiful wish to bestow upon me but there are no words to describe what your sacrifice, your love, your prayers, and your covering has done for me, my family, and the community I serve. This is a small token of gratitude for all the peace, clarity, love, and esteem that has grown from your works. Thank you for all that you are, all that you have done, all that you will do.

Introduction

This Build Yourself Up journal started with a desire for self discovery. I was challenged by my life coach to become curious about myself. Rather than looking deeply into anything and everyone else, I was told to put all that energy into me, my desires, recognizing my own emotions, and triggers. To recognize my own wants and needs. In the midst of that, I felt the shift. I felt a confidence. I saw a change in how I treated my husband, my children, and my friends.

Instead of looking outward at everyone else, my circumstances, my environment, and the world around me. I went in.

This Build Yourself Up Journal is challenging you to look. If you want to transform your circumstances, shift your energy towards your partner, and your children, redefine and better yourself in the space of partner, mother, and friend, then you have to go within. This journal was crafted to help you do that. Perhaps you originally thought they should be the one to change, but you have learned you can't control them. You can only control you. Perhaps you want to change how you see them, how you experience them, how you interact with them. In learning to control yourself, your emotions, your thoughts, and your habits, you will show up as your best, and everyone else will benefit. This journal will help you to recover that control.

Often times we want to improve ourselves so that we can show up better for other people. So that we can give more, pour more, do more, and expand our reach. We have been taught to pour out into others and to fill ourselves back up. I have learned through many works, books, aunties, grandmothers, colleagues, friends, and self discovery that too much is required of us, for us to spill out. We have to move from a space of pouring and move to a space of overflow. So instead we will improve ourselves for ourselves and everyone else may benefit from this progress that we have made. Do this for you. Do this because you want to, because you deserve it.

We need to get so full that people don't get us, they get what runneth over. We are so deserving of the abundance of spirit, love, joy, peace, patience, kindness, goodness, faithfulness, gentleness, and self-control.

This Build Yourself Up Journal is so that you don't have to turn to your favorite podcast, your favorite IG account, your favorite playlist, your spouse, your children, or your friends. You turn to God, you turn to you. And you use your own words to give you life.

Happy filling. Welcome to The Overflow.

How To Use

The prompts in the journal range in length and depth. Each prompt is built on the two principles in Social Emotional Learning of Self-Awareness and Self-Management. Before we can focus on our interactions with others, we must first focus on our interaction with self.

It is *encouraged* that you *discuss your revelation* with a close friend, a partner, or a family member that you enjoy. This journal is meant to tap into you as the woman before the wife and the mother. Relish in that. *This journal is time for you.*

Try to take this in **during quiet time**, when you can have **10 minutes or so alone** and in best practice not when you are in a rush, or right before you get into something else. This journal is a time for self reflection, self discovery, and the peeling of the unnecessary.

Contents

Contents

Contents

If I didn't define myself for myself, I would be crunched into other people's fantasies for me and eaten alive.

- Audre Lorde

Affirmations

Often people know what they are, but rarely do they get into the habit of using them daily.

Affirmations are statements that are meant to empower and build up your subconscious and conscious mind. These statements are intended to be words you would use to describe a state of being that you want to achieve. Normally they are short, and often times that can be in disagreement with what you know to be true.

The point of an affirmation to get to the feeling of being or having, to then change your thoughts, which then change your decisions, which then change your behavior, which then change your habits, which then change your life.

You speak in a positive manner, refrain from don't, won't, or not, and then you will have your affirmations.

Affirmation List

Affirmations: Write as many as you need. Instead of saying, "I don't feel stressed" you would say I feel calm.

Your Perfect Day

Life is too short to live the life you have to. Every day you get to make a choice. So think like you have the freedom to choose. With these questions in mind, outline your perfect day.

What happens in your perfect morning? What time do you wake up? What does your room look like? What does your bed feel like? What do you wear? What do you do first thing? What do you have for breakfast? What do you do with your kids? What do you do with the rest of your morning? Who do you talk to? How do you feel? Describe in as much detail as you can.

What time do you have for lunch? What do you eat? Where are you? What do you do after lunch? How do you spend your afternoon? What do you for yourself? What do you and the kids do? How do you feel?

Perfect Day Continued

What time do you eat dinner? What do you eat? What do you and the family do after dinner? What time do the kids go to bed? What do you do when the kids are down for bed? What do you do with the remainder of your day? How do you feel at the end of the day?

Think about what you can add to your days right now to make it more like your perfect day.

Remove Your Titles

Who are you outside of your titles, labels, occupation, and relationships to others. While relationships, jobs, and interests are important, using them for self definition becomes a problem when things change. When you change jobs, when beautiful things come to a end. Who you are OUTSIDE of these things define how you show up to those titles, labels, and occupation. So take a moment an think, who are you? Think back to your affirmations.

What do you value?

CIRCLE WHAT RESONATES

Kindness
Integrity
Creativity
Learning
Family
Growth
Religion
Authenticity
Health
Beauty
Wealth
Generosity
Justice
Fun
Popularity
Humility
Open Mindedness

CIRCLE WHAT RESONATES

Success
Achievement
Influence
Leadership
Competition
Hard Work
Gratitude
Adventure
Security
Respect
Commitment
Free Time
Relaxation
Responsibility
Independence
Teamwork
Freedom
Service to Others

Other Values Not Listed:

True North

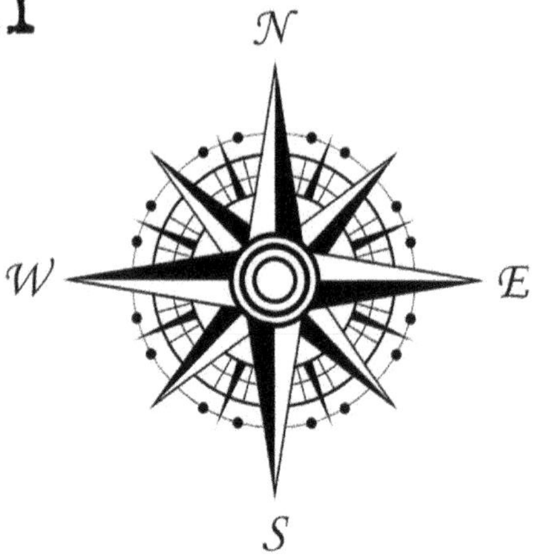

What are your top values?

What are some of the ways that they show up in your daily life?

How could you narrow down your values to 3? What 3 values do you care to live by?

Interests

"Interest-
the state of wanting to know or learn about something or someone"

What are some of the things that you shown interest in? Think of all the things you can and list below

Passions

Passion-
a strong interest or desire;
something that gives you
boundless energy, focus,
and willpower.

Passions are things that are far more interesting that your interests. These are the things that get you stuck, that you feel serious interest about, that you can talk about for hours. Take a look at this list and try and be specific. If its cooking. Then think, what style of cooking, what ingredients, what flavors? What is it that you know a lot about and still want to know more? Now, fill the list as honestly as you can. You will use this later on how to fill yourself up.

What are some of the things that you shown interest in? Think of all the things you can and list below

____
____
____
____
____
____
____
____
____
____
____
____
____
____
____
____
____
____
____
____

10 Year Reflection

What did your life look like 10 years ago? Think: How old, where did you live, who were you with, what did you do for a living, how much did you have in the bank, what had you accomplished, what were your set backs, how did you overcome, what were your values, what were your fears, what were your goals around this time?

5 Year Reflection

What did your life look like 5 years agoThink: How old, where did you live, who were you with, what did you do for a living, how much did you have in the bank, what had you accomplished, what were your set backs, how did you overcome, what were your values, what were your fears, what were your goals around this time?

1 Year Reflection

What did your life look like 1 years agoThink: How old, where did you live, who were you with, what did you do for a living, how much did you have in the bank, what had you accomplished, what were your set backs, how did you overcome, what were your values, what were your fears, what were your goals around this time?

Progress

Social media would have you to believe that things happen over night. How different is your life from 10, 5, and 1 year ago, on a scale of 1 to 10, 10 being extremely different, 1 being the same, 5 being a mid way point?

Circle a number for each year span

10 years ago? 1 2 3 4 5 6 7 8 9 10

5 years ago? 1 2 3 4 5 6 7 8 9 10

1 year ago? 1 2 3 4 5 6 7 8 9 10

Are you happy with your changes over this time? Why or why not?

Where does your family, and friends, fit into your changes these past 10 years? Where they the cause, were they impacted by it, or did they get to see it?

Your Point of View

Finish this sentence. Life is ______________________________

How does this idea affect your view of life?

How does this idea affect your view of family?

How does this idea affect your view of employment?

How does this idea affect your view of your kids?

How does this idea affect your view of your romantic relationship?

Check in

Check to see if you agree or disagree with the following statements. After completing this section:

I have affirmations to build myself up.
I can explain my perfect day in great detail.
I can describe myself outside of
the roles that I have.
I know what my top values are?
I know what your interests are?
I know what your passions are?
I can pinpoint how I feel about the changes in my life
from 10 years ago.
from 5 years ago.
from 1 year ago.
I can see how your life view impacts my view of myself?
I can see how your life view impacts view of my family.
I can see how your life view impacts view of my employment.
I can see how your life view impacts view of my kids.
I can see how your life view impacts view of my romantic relationship.

If you answered, "disagree" to any of the previous statements please go back to the page aligning with the question and complete the page more thoroughly. If no additional insight comes. then continue working on the upcoming pages and revisit at a later time.

The Feelings Wheel

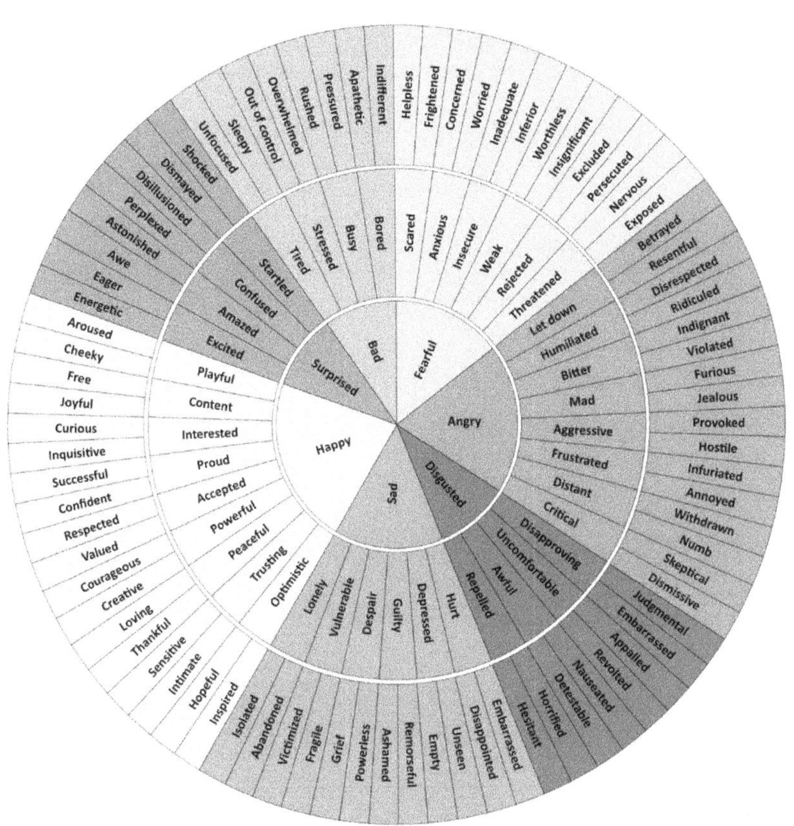

Credit: (Geoffrey Roberts) for attribution. of Whitehouse Church

Use this visual to better discuss your feelings. Attach the feeling to the word that best describes it.

Feelings Tracker

Make note of how you feel each day. Try Tracking at 2 or 3 times of the day. What do you notice? What do you wonder? Are there any changes that need to be made?

			1	2
3	4	5	6	7
8	9	10	11	12
13	14	15	16	17
18	19	20	21	22
23	24	25	26	27
28	29	30	31	

My Feelings

Identify some situations, people, places, and things that bring about these feelings for you.

Happy	
Sad	
Disgust	
Anger	
Fear	

Set the Mood

When you are in a good mood how do your partner and your children typically behave or react?

How does this typically make you feel? Seeing their reaction to your feelings and emotions?

What is your family's reaction when you are angry or sad?

Set the Mood Continued

Is your family's reaction to your sadness and anger the response the you want? Why or why not?

A mother is the first teacher. The first role model of how to manage emotions, frustrations, feelings of joy and excitement. Knowing the power that you have and the impact you may have on your family, does this make you want to show more or less emotion? Why or why not?

Giving our children the language to communicate their feelings and their emotions can help them in the long run when interacting with people outside of the home. It is not enough for your child to simply say sad. Depending on the age, what other words for the basic feelings can you introduce to your children to express more complex emotions. Write them below.

Love On Yourself

Take 5 minutes and compliment yourself on who you are, how you look, what you have on, your energy, your vibe, your personality, etc. Ready? Set? Go!

Strengths

What are some of the things that you are naturally good at, you do with ease, or maybe in an area that you often get compliments for? Think of your personal and professional strengths. Try and list 4 in each category. Areas that you would rate yourself a 9-10 on a scale of 10?

How do those strengths show up with your partner, family, and friends?

How do those strengths show up in your work place, in your community, or in other areas of your life?

Limits

What are some of the tasks and activities that you struggle with, some of the things that see you would rate yourself as a 5-6 on a scale of 10?

How do those limits show up with your partner, family, and friends?

When do you ever shown resentment towards your limitations?

Strengths Revisited

When have you show frustrations towards other who share the same strengths as you?

When have you shown frustrations towards others who share the same limits as you?

When have you shown frustrations towards others who have a strength in areas where you are limited?

Motivation

Motivation is the reason or reasons behind someone's actions and behavior. Really it is your reason why. Often times, we don't activate or move ourselves towards the things we want because the reason why is not compelling enough. What's your reason?

Why are you doing any of this? Why do you wake up in the morning? What do you want your days to be filled with? Why are you working in your career, living where you live? What will this all mean? What are you hoping to have your life mean in the end? Are you living in a rush? Are you living like you have all the time in the world? And if you did how would you want to spend it? Why are you doing any of this? Your life, your career, your kids, your family, your choices?

What is Your Why?

Beauty

What are your favorite adjectives to describe your beauty?

What are some of your favorite features?

How do you accentuate them? How could you accentuate them more?

Check In

See if you agree or disagree with the following statements.

I can identify what makes me happy, sad, disgusted, angry, and fearful.

I can can see how my mood impacts my family.

I can use more feeling words into my and my child's vocabulary.

I can see the beauty in myself.

I can identify my strengths.

I can identify my limits.

I see clearly how I treat others who have the same limits or strengths as me.

I can call on my motivation at will.

I can compliment myself.

If you disagreed with any of the previous statements, please go back and complete the page that aligns to the statement more thoroughly. If you are out of answers continue through the journal and circle back when you feel more prepared to answer.

We don't pour out.
We overflow into
everyone else and the
roles in life we play.
How are you filling
yourself up?

Fill Up

You can't pour from an empty cup. What are some ways that you fill yourself up? How do you pour into yourself to overflow into your family, friends, and community? (Things that bring you joy, excite you, restore you, calm you?

Trinkets

What are things you love to get randomly from others?

Your Turn

Go get yourself one of those things in the next 48 hours.
What did you get yourself?

Looking Your Best

Often times we save "looking our best" for a special night out, special occasions, birthdays and celebration. We buy the outfit, the shoes, the statement piece for fill in the blank. Instead, let's try this on. Get our hair done, nails done, make up, perfumes or the likes for just the everyday.

How about creating a special every day Looking My Best even when going to work, even just to the store, even just around the house.

What would you everyday Looking My Best look and feel like?

Change Clothes

Think about your current wardrobe. Does it excite you? Do you feel amazing when you put your pieces on? Think about a revamp? What do you want to wear more of? Think color, clothing item, brand, and style.

So what will you wear tomorrow!

Self Care

If we put in as many hours of self care as we did working, cooking, cleaning, etc. What all would you do? What are some of the ways you practice self-care? What else could you do to practice self -care if you had more time. Take 5 minutes to fill out your list

Self Care Should Occur Daily.

Plan Out Your Self Care for the week after taking a look at some more ideas to help restore yourself so that your cup is full.

30 More Ways to Show Self Care

1. Write a Brain Dump to clear your mind
2. Clean up your space
3. Buy the book
4. Get creative
5. Play your favorite board game
6. Wear that outfit you have been saving
7. Call up a good friend
8. Have your favorite beverage
9. Go for a walk
10. Play your favorite playlist
11. Go for a drive and let the windows down
12. Go for a hike
13. Wear your favorite piece of clothing
14. Say no to something you don't want to do
15. Say yes to something you know you want to do
16. Take a nap
17. Identify your triggers and manage your emotions
18. Take a social media break
19. Catch up on your favorite show
20. Pick up some new candles
21. Say your affirmations
22. Write in your journal
23. Make your favorite treat
24. Get your nails done
25. Pray
26. Clean out your closet
27. Give yourself a facial
28. Add some essential oils to your diffuser
29. Have some tea
30. Meditate

Now go back, what can you add to your list.

Gratitude

A grateful heart creates joy and peace. In the midsts or working and climbing and moving to the next time, being grateful requires that you practice mindfulness of the present moment, and appreciate where you are and what you have. This is yet another obvious activity but take 5 minutes and write down things you are grateful for.

Your willingness

to look at your darkness,

is what empowers

you to change

- Iyanla Vanzant

Triggers

Everyone has their own individual triggers. Being able to identify what triggers you is the starting point to calmer days and less frustrations.

Emotional State	
People	
Places	
Situations	
Other	

Unpack Your Trigger Pt. 1

Think of a situation, argument, or scenario that led to you being upset, frustrated, angry or hurt. What happened? How did you feel?

Why was that important?

Continue onto the next page!

Unpack Your Trigger Pt. 2

And, Why was that important?

And, Why was that important?

And, Why was that important?

Continue onto the next page!

Unpack Your Trigger Pt. 3

What you have likely come to is the root of the problem to what you are feeling and why you are triggered. Typically it takes 5 whys but you may have gotten there sooner. What can you do now with the information behind why you were triggered? What can you do in the future to work through the root of why you are triggered?

Trauma

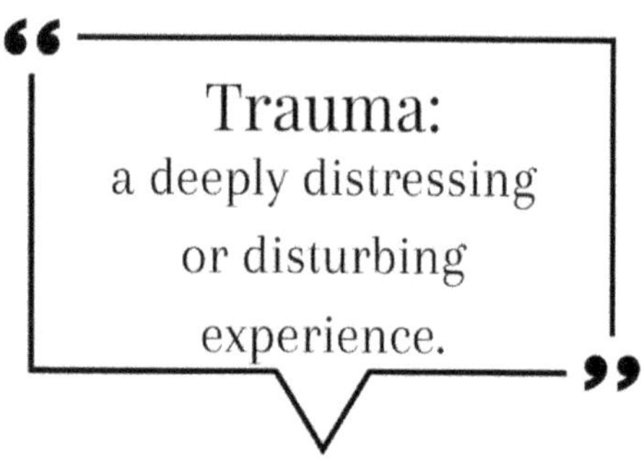

It typically involves the loss of control, betrayal, abuse of power, helplessness, pain, confusion and/or loss. Sometimes it life altering at other points its life halting.

While your trauma may be a part of your story and your overall testimony for how you made it through, what would be the play book for how you made it. How you transformed after the your healing? The badge isn't in what you endured, the badge of honor is who you became after you went through what you went through.

It is not enough to simply address it and then dismiss your feelings. Depending upon what this brings up for you it may be necessary to just journal and go on about your day. Our healing may require counseling, education, medication, or other necessary supports depending on your own individual discretion. You know better than anyone what you may or may not need. Trust your instincts.

Additional ways to cope with thinking and perhaps relieving your trauma try some of these strategies:

- Take 5 deep breaths inhaling and exhaling on a 5 count
- Validate your experience
- Ground yourself by focusing on your 5 senses to remind yourself that you are where your feet are
- Think of something that makes you laugh

Other Side of Trauma?

Trauma, Negative Labels & Bad Experiences	Healed Version of Yourself

Worry

What are some of the things that you worry about? Make a list here.

Your attitude
Your words
Your effort
Your responses
Your tone
Your time
Your interest
Your arrival
Your preparation
Your soothing

After reviewing the Locus of Control, the things that are within your capacity to change, go back and cross every worry off of your list that is outside of your control.

Worry Continued

"Worry doesn't take away tomorrow's problems, it takes away today's peace."

Now for the things that are still on your list. Pick 1 worry that you can create a solution for.

How Do You Cope?

What are some of the ways you deal with stress, anxiety, frustration, anger, and burn out?

COPE

Continue onto next page

Ways to Help You Cope

1. Take 5 deep breaths
2. Identify the opportunities that are present
3. Count backwards from 10
4. Center yourself by restating your affirmation
5. Take a break
6. Ask for help
7. Go for a walk
8. Use positive self-talk
9. Think of something that makes you happy
10. Drink some water
11. Meditate
12. Seek advice from a trusted advisor
13. Set a short term goal
14. Write down your thoughts
15. Stretch
16. Take a bath
17. Rate the size of your problem 1-3
18. Cry
19. Identify what is in your control
20. Acknowledge your feelings
21. Do a gratitude exercise
22. Express your frustrations
23. Advocate for what you need in the moment
24. Exercise
25. Vent to a close friend

Pick 3 things to help yourself cope with your day today.

Plan to Cope

What are some ways you are going to better include relaxation into your days to better help you cope?

What time can you set aside? How long?

Now put a reminder in your phone. Create an event in your calendar. Tell your partner and friends so that they can hold you accountable. Which steps did you take? List them down.

Check In

Identify if you agree or disagree with the following statements.

I know how to fill myself up.
I know what trinkets to get myself to brighten my day.
I have your own personal definition for looking my best.
I know what I love to wear to feel good.
I have ways to practice self care.
I have ways to practice gratitude.
I can identify what my triggers are.
I have a way to unpack my triggers.
I can see a version of myself beyond my past traumas.
I have a way to cope with my worries.

If you answered, "disagree" to any of the previous statements please go back to the page aligning with the question and complete the page more thoroughly. If no additional insight comes. then continue working on the upcoming pages and revisit at a later time.

"As you become more clear on who you really are, you'll be better able to decide what is best for you, the first time around"

-Oprah Winfrey

What's Your Communication Style?

Choose the most appropriate response to the following statements:

	Strongly Agree	Agree	Disagree	Strongly Disagree
I often say things without thinking about the consequences of my words.	◯	◯	◯	◯
I have a reputation for speaking my mind.	◯	◯	◯	◯
I question people about their basic beliefs and opinions.	◯	◯	◯	◯
When I feel like I am being attacked I shut down	◯	◯	◯	◯
I feel comfortable sharing the things that interest me	◯	◯	◯	◯
I feel more comfortable when other people do most of the talking and sharing of themselves.	◯	◯	◯	◯
I don't like to discuss my romantic relationships.	◯	◯	◯	◯
I don't talk easily tio strangers	◯	◯	◯	◯

What's Your Communication Style: Survey Continued?

Choose the most appropriate response to the following statements:

	Strongly Agree	Agree	Disagree	Strongly Disagree
I tend to worry about how I present myself when I am speaking	○	○	○	○
I hate being interrupted during a conversation	○	○	○	○
I struggle in not interrupting people during a conversation or disagreement	○	○	○	○
I speak for my partner during group conversations	○	○	○	○
I allow my partner to speak for me	○	○	○	○
When we are upset I don't think we should be responsible for things we say	○	○	○	○
When I am upset due to an argument just give me time to cool down.	○	○	○	○
I think it's appropriate to leave when you feel you are getting upset during a difficult conversation	○	○	○	○

Review Your Communication

What about your answers to the survey surprised you?

What about your answers to the survey seemed obvious you?

What do you feel are some of the things you do well when you communicate?

What do you want to do different regarding how you communicate?

Affective Statements

To move from combative and defensive language in disagreements we have to move from a place of judgement and assessment of others' actions to a place of observation and checking in on what we need in those moments from others to feel safe and secure in those relationships. Rather than creating a story of what we think is happening behind the actions, the words, the decisions, we need to step back and take in only what we see. So think of a recent disagreement or miscommunication. Try using the frame to get to a solution rather than creating further distance between you and the person.

When I see/hear you play the game all day and night
I feel lonely
because I have a need for connection.
Would you be willing to take a break after dinner to watch a show with me?

Use This Template

When I see/hear ______________________________

I feel ____

because I have a need for ______________________

Would you be willing to ______________________?

Outward- In

What are some qualities that you want in your partners?

What are some qualities that you want in your children?

Habits, behaviors, and tendencies that we are most critical of in others are mainly because we are critical of them in ourselves. So instead of looking outward, try looking in. How can you show those same qualities in yourself to serve as a model to your family.

Good Mother

What does the world say a good mother is?

What do YOU say a good mother is?

What About Your Mom?

What are some of the things your mom did as a child that you enjoyed?

What are some of the things your mom did as a child that you hated?

Something to think about: What are some ways you are avoiding following those same bad habits with your own children?

Motherhood

What is the end goal for your motherhood? How do you want your children to turn out? How do you want to feel when they are all grown up with families of their own?

When I Heard Them Say

What do you want your kids to say about you when they get older? List 10 things you wish could over hear them say.

How would you feel to hear them say this?

What are some things you can do today so that they may say these things? Go do them now.

Talk About Them

How would you describe your child to someone else? List 7 things.

How many of those things were negative? ____ (or how many did you think and not write down)

For every negative statement you need 5 positive statements to neutralize it, for the statement not to have an impact on them. So in reality you need 6 positive statements just to fill your child back up. Now, for every 1 negative statement. Write 5 positive ones about your child.

Continue here if need be.

This applies to every interaction, every criticism, every critique, every put down, or flare up, negative comment, or acts of disrespect. Take a moment to think, how often are you filling your family up?

Good Partner

What does the world say a good wife is?	What do YOU say a good wife is?

Be The Partner You Want

What are the things you want in your partner?

Become so that you can attract the behaviors, actions, ideas, and demeanors that you want? How can you work to be more of those things?

The Partner You Want Continued

The things that we are most hard on our partner about are the things that we are most hard on ourselves about? How does that fit into your current frustrations with your partner?

Knowing you are being hard on yourself, what are some ways you can lighten up?

Value Circle

Who are the 5 people you spend the most time with?

List them in terms of the top values you have. How do they fit?

Person	Value

Are there any persons who you spend the most time with that don't fit into the values you hold for yourself?

If your answer is no then, great! You know that your circle is tight. If your answer is yes, then consider what they may bring to you that you do value. The idea is not to end relationships or to throw someone away. The idea is to be in alignment and true to yourself and the things you value and desire.

Your Mentors

You don't have to know everything. It is often advised against. It's more than enough to be good at 1 or 2 things but be able to find an answer for everything. Mentors, whether they are people you know personally, or figures that you can go to through books, social media, podcasts, etc. to help you navigate your problems. Identify them with this list below

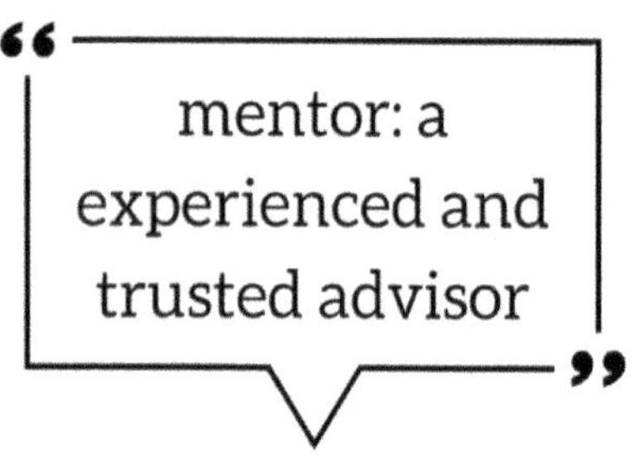

Area of Life	Mentor Name	How do you access this person? Online/In Person
Spirituality		
Health		
Marriage/ Relationships		
Family		
Career		
Recreation/Leisure		
Education		
Finance		
Environment/Community		

"If you can not see where you are going, ask someone who has been before"

J - Loren Norris

Qualified Mentors

Area of Life: Spirituality

Mentor: ___________________

What qualifies this person to be a mentor in this area of life?

Area of Life: Health

Mentor: ___________________

What qualifies this person to be a mentor in this area of life?

Area of Life: Relationships/Family

Mentor: ___________________

What qualifies this person to be a mentor in this area of life?

Area of Life: Career

Mentor: ___________________

What qualifies this person to be a mentor in this area of life?

Qualified Mentors Cont.

Area of Life: Recreation/Leisure

Mentor: __________________

What qualifies this person to be a mentor in this area of life?

Area of Life: Education

Mentor: __________________

What qualifies this person to be a mentor in this area of life?

Area of Life: Finance

Mentor: __________________

What qualifies this person to be a mentor in this area of life?

Area of Life: Community

Mentor: __________________

What qualifies this person to be a mentor in this area of life?

Consistency

Consistent: acting or done in the same way over time. Reaching our goals are rooted in being consistent and not so much inspiration or habit.

What are 10 things you do consistently over the course of a week?

You are the collection of ideas, behaviors, habits, and beliefs that you do consistently. What is 1 thing you want to do more of?

Habits

List of some of your habits so that we can build out a new habit that you want to form.

Good Habits	Bad Habits

Looking at your bad habits, what is one habit that you want to change? What can you do to REPLACE that habit over the next 21 days?

For example: I tend to sip a glass of wine at night to relax after I put the kids down for bed. Instead of wine, I swap it out for tea.

Another example: Would be, after having lunch I would feel tired and go have a nap. Instead, I switched out a nap and went for a walk. No more mid-day sleeping.

Pick 1 bad habit that you want to replace?

____

____

What will you do to replace the habit?

____

____

____

What is your new habit?

____

____

____

Habit Tracker

To build a habit you need to do it everyday for 21 days for it to stick. It takes 30 days to become a lifestyle. It is best for you to do it at the same time everyday. Pick 1 NEW habit to track.

			1	2
3	4	5	6	7
8	9	10	11	12
13	14	15	16	17
18	19	20	21	22
23	24	25	26	27
28	29	30	31	

Favorite Quotes

What are some of your favorite quotes that you love to live by? Write down or look up 6 that you can refer to when things get difficult, so that you can carry on.

Quote 1

Quote 2

Quote 3

Favorite Quotes

What are some of your favorite quotes that you love to live by? Write down or look up 6 that you can refer to when things get difficult, so that you can carry on.

Quote 4

Quote 5

Quote 6

Check In

Identify if you agree or disagree with the following statements.

I know how I tend to communicate with others
I know how to communicate what I need from others.
I can identify the traits and habits I want in myself.
I have my own definition for what it means to be a good mother to live up to.
I know ways I want to improve my own mother child relationships with my own children.
I have a clear vision for what I want my motherhood to offer my children and myself.
I can describe my child in positive and affirming ways.
I have my own definition of what it means to be a good wife to live up to.
I know the habits that I want in myself as a partner.
I know how my circle of people that reflect my alignment & values.
I have a list of qualified mentors to go to for every area in life.
I have a way of being consistent with my good habits
I have my own go to quotes and saying to pour into myself.

If you answered, "disagree" to any of the previous statements please go back to the page aligning with the question and complete the page more thoroughly. If no additional insight comes. then continue working on the upcoming pages and revisit at a later time.

Gratitude Repeated

Set a timer for 5 minutes. Write down a list of all the things you are grateful for:

Is your list abstract (in theory) or tangible (physical or an item)? Take a moment and think why do you think that is ?

Continue onto the next page!

Gratitude Continued

How far down the list did you write in your own name?

Why do you think that is?

Who are you without you? What can you be grateful for about you?

Persevere

Failure can be devastating. There can be times when you feel like you are trying for something and it is out of reach. Recall a time when you persevered and continued on. A time when you failed at something but eventually accomplished your goal. How did you feel? What did you learn about yourself?

Birthing

List some of the things you have birthed into existence outside of your children. Being pregnant means to be full of meaning, suggestive, or significant. Think in terms of your career, your degrees, your business, your awards, your skills, etc.

What are some things that you want to bring about in your future? List them here.

Living Beyond Fear

You can do absolutely anything. You can think your way through every problem. You can find a path through every thicket. How would you know? Show yourself below.

Currently, what is one of your biggest goals that you have for yourself ?

What's the worse thing that could happen if you were to pursue your next big goal?

How would you fix it, what could you do to get yourself out of the situation?

Bucket List

Start a bucket list of the things you want to do THIS YEAR. Not things that you may be able to do but somethings you really want to do!

Pick 1 thing you can do in the next 60 days.

Plan it out on the next page

MY BUCKET LIST EVENT PLAN

DATE(S) SCHEDULED

HOW MUCH WILL COST?

LUNCH:

WHO WILL GO: ____________________

WHERE TO:

WHAT TIMES:

HOW WILL YOU TRAVEL THERE?

THINGS TO-DO BEFORE THE EVENT

- ○
- ○
- ○
- ○
- ○
- ○
- ○

NOTES:

THINGS YOU NEED TO GET

- __________
- __________
- __________
- __________
- __________
- __________
- __________
- __________
- __________
- __________

HOW WILL YOU COMMEMORATE IT?

- ○ post on social media
- ○ grab a souvenir
- ○ create a memory box
- ○ send a postcard
- ○ scrapbook page

Success is

liking yourself,

liking what you do,

and

liking how you do it.

- Maya Angelou

Success Defined

Describe the big picture. Using a word of expression, finish the sentence.

In my personal life, success is ______________________________

In my family life, success is ________________________________

In my romantic relationship
success is, ____

In my spiritual life, success is ______________________________

In my career, success is ___________________________________

In my recreation, success is _________________________________

In my self care, success is __________________________________

For my finances, success is _________________________________

Success is ____

"Don't sit down and wait for the opportunities to come.

Get up and make them."

Madame C. J. Walker

Success

What is your personal recipe for success? What has served you in the past? What can you do more of in the future?

Goal Planner

Specific	Measurable	Attainable	Relevant	Time Bound
The goal is detailed, singular, and clearly stated.	*Create numbers for it so that you can track progress and growth*	*Be honest, what can you attain with the time, energy, and resources.*	*Make sure it aligns with your values and long term goals.*	*Give yourself a date to have it done by. Think short term within the next year.*

Nonexample: *I will lose weight.*

Example: *By 11/25/2021, I will lose 20 pounds by eating 3 fruits and vegetables every day and working out 3 times a week, so I can feel better and keep up with my kids during their activities.*

Create Your Goal

Specific	
Measurable	
Attainable	
Relevant	
Time Bound	

Identify 3 Checkpoints for you to get to your main goal.

#1 Checkpoint	
#2 Checkpoint	
#3 Checkpoint	

Letter to Your Future Self

The best way to predict the future is to create it. To lean into your intuition, your power, and your resolve. Lean into what is already there for you to receive. Throughout this journey you have chiseled away some challenges and built up areas of your self-esteem, your strengths, your self - efficacy, your wants. With this in mind, write a letter to yourself. Talk about what you have accomplished, your dreams, your partner, your children, your friendships, and yourself. Write this letter to your future self, identifying was is listed below. Return to this a year from today.

Letter to Yourself Continued

Check In

Identify if you agree or disagree with the following statements.

I can practice gratitude and know I am my best thing.
I can pull on past experiences that I have thrived in to encourage myself.
I can list out my accomplishments to show myself I can do whatever I push myself to do.
I can work my way out of difficult circumstances.
I have a list of things that I REALLY want to do, see, and be.
I can create a clear plan to get what I want done.
I have my own personal definition for success.
I know what it takes to be successful.
I know how to set out a plan to accomplish my goals.

If you answered, "disagree" to any of the previous statements please go back to the page aligning with the question and complete the page more thoroughly. If no additional insight comes. then continue working on the upcoming pages and revisit at a later time.

"You are your best thing."

-Toni Morrison

Notes

Notes

Notes

About the Author

Sheamonique Tracey is a wife, mom, and mentor. She is a Social Emotional Learning Coach and Advocate. She earned her bachelor's degree in Africana Studies from San Diego State University and her Master's Special Education from National University and has worked as an educator for the past 6 years helping students and families in the areas of communication, SEL, executive skills, and personal development.

www.sheatracey.com

Terms of Use

This product is for personal use. Please respect the time and effort put into this project by not sharing. Additional licenses can be purchased from my store at a slightly discounted rate.

Disclaimer: These resources and materials are for supplementary support/education purchases and are not intended to be a replacement for counseling, education, medication, or other necessary supports.

www.sheatracey.com

www.ingramcontent.com/pod-product-compliance
Ingram Content Group UK Ltd.
Pitfield, Milton Keynes, MK11 3LW, UK
UKHW020239250726
13967UKWH00001B/449